HELPING

Photographs by James Levin

Edited by Jackie Carter

SCHOLASTIC INC.
NEW YORK TORONTO LONDON AUCKLAND SYDNEY

To all of the children, families, and teachers who helped to make this book possible.

Library of Congress Cataloging-in-Publication Data

Levin, James, date-
   Helping / photographs by James Levin; edited by Jackie Carter.
         p. cm — (My first library)
      Summary: Labeled photographs portray children helping at home,
at school, and in the community by such acts as sweeping, weeding, and fixing.
      ISBN 0-590-49293-4   ISBN 0-590-29269-2 (meets NASTA specifications)
      1. Helping behavior — Juvenile literature. [Helpfulness.
2. Vocabulary.] I. Carter, Jackie, date-   . II. Title. III. Series.
BF637.H4L48 1993
177'.7—dc20   92-41613
                                   CIP
                                   AC

Copyright © 1993 by Scholastic Inc.
Photographs copyright © 1993 James Levin
Designed by Bill SMITH STUDIO, Inc.
All rights reserved. Published by Scholastic Inc.
My First Library is a registered trademark of Scholastic Inc.
   2 3 4 5 6 7 8 9 10   09   01 00 99 98 97 96 95 94
Printed in the U.S.A.
First Scholastic printing, 1993

Acknowledgments: Special thanks to the children, teachers, directors, and parents at the
Country Children's Center in Katonah, N.Y., Merricat's Castle School, and Cardinal
Spellman Head Start in New York City, who welcomed us into their schools and homes
to take the beautiful photographs that appear in this book. Thanks also to Lisa Feeney,
La Famiglia Restaurant, and the Cross River Pharmacy in Cross River, N.Y.

Helping...

Dressing

sweeping

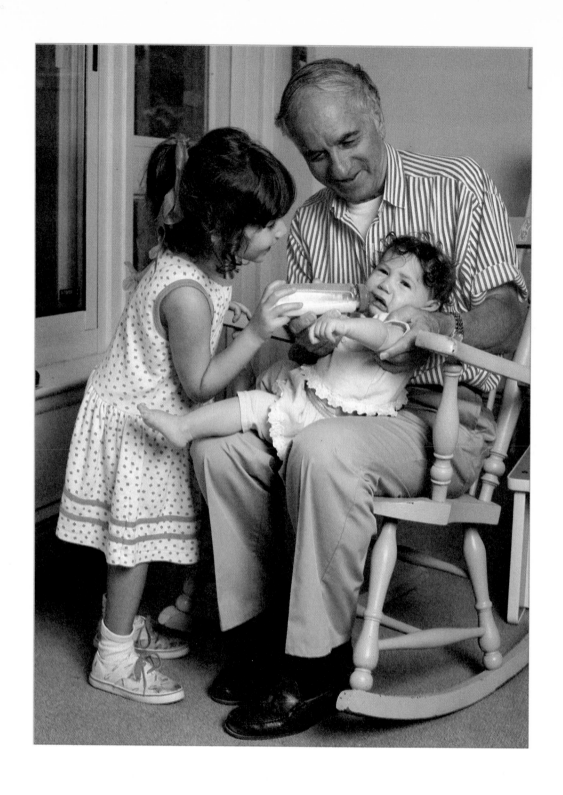

caring

feeding...

tying

shopping

stepping

weeding...

Pushing

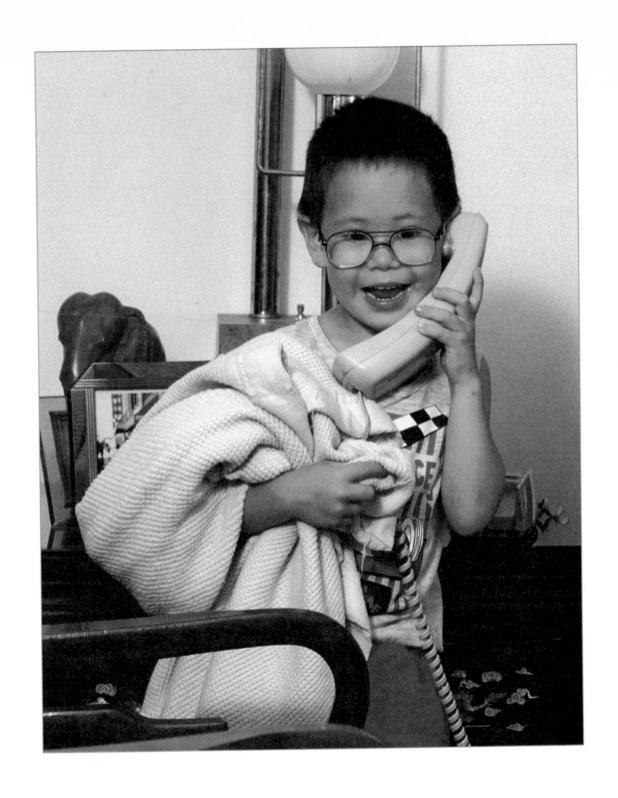

answering

folding

stacking...

wiping

buckling

mailing

snacking…

Washing

watering

sliding

fixing...

picking

peeling

pouring

mixing...

Hammering

tossing

almost done...

inside, outside... helping's fun!

Helping

Dressing, sweeping,
caring, feeding;
tying, shopping,
stepping, weeding.

Pushing, answering,
folding, stacking;
wiping, buckling,
mailing, snacking.

Washing, watering,
sliding, fixing;
picking, peeling,
pouring, mixing.

Hammering, tossing...
almost done;
inside, outside...
helping's fun!